Praise for *Enough*

T0013884

"Scott Stabile is one of the wisest [...] wisdom earned from his experience in practicing being [...] as he is. He's who I call when I have forgotten who I am or why I'm here or what the point of any of life is — and that's what *Enough as You Are* is. It is Scott in your pocket reminding you of the exact things that you have forgotten, that you need to remember, especially right now when the whole world seems to have forgotten. This book is a treasure, a manual, a daily prayer."
— **Holly Whitaker**, *New York Times* bestselling author of
Quit Like a Woman

"Build yourself a temple of these pages and go there as often as you can. Book a spa day there. Do it until your belief in each message is as rooted and immutable as an oak tree, and you will have done yourself the greatest kindness. And in so doing, you'll have done a great kindness for all the world."
— **Lisa McCourt**, author of *Free Your Joy*
and founder of Joy School

"Do you need to remember that you — not some phantom better version of you, but the exact you reading these words — are enough? This book will help with that. And in the process, you will feel more capable of creating the life you've always longed for. Not just more capable, though ... let this book fall on your awareness like gentle rain, bringing a powerful truth into focus: you are worthy, you are enough, you are loved."
— **Jacob Nordby**, author of *The Creative Cure:
How Finding and Freeing Your Inner Artist Can Heal Your Life*

"*Enough as You Are* is not just a book — it is the GPS for our hearts and our souls and, yes, our collective humanity. I found myself sobbing when I read, 'It's just that empathy invites a connection that sympathy simply can't.' Every single human being needs to read this book. No exceptions. This book, this exquisite gem, will pry open even the most stubborn heart. It was an honor to be invited to read this, a true honor."
— **Amy Ferris**, author of *Mighty Gorgeous:
A Little Book about Messy Love*

ENOUGH AS YOU ARE

Also by Scott Stabile

*Big Love: The Power of Living
with a Wide-Open Heart*

Just Love

Iris

ENOUGH AS YOU ARE

SCOTT STABILE

New World Library
Novato, California

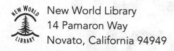

New World Library
14 Pamaron Way
Novato, California 94949

Text design by Tona Pearce Myers

Library of Congress Cataloging-in-Publication data is available.

First printing, October 2023

ISBN 978-1-60868-896-8
Ebook ISBN 978-1-60868-897-5
Printed in Canada on 100% postconsumer-waste recycled paper

New World Library is proud to be a Gold Certified Environmentally Responsible Publisher. Publisher certification awarded by Green Press Initiative.

10   9   8   7   6   5   4   3   2   1

For Goran, my all-time favorite

Contents

Author's Note • x

You • 1

Me • 71

Us • 141

About the Author • 221

Author's Note

I'm really excited you've picked up this book. I'm confident that as you make your way through these pages, you will feel understood, embraced, respected, and seen. Maybe not on every page but often enough to keep you reading. My hope is that you will also feel worthy, loved, and enough, as you are. That is my hope for us all.

A friend once referred to me as a love activist, and that's a title I happily own. I don't see myself as an expert in anything, but I am pretty damn good at loving myself, which naturally translates into good love for others too. I believe love to be our most powerful force for real, lasting healing, and that a dedication to self-love is the most important commitment we can make for ourselves and our world. This book is an expression of my belief in the potential within each of us to recognize our imperfect humanity and decide, no matter what, to accept and love ourselves still.

That sounds good, doesn't it? It *is* possible.

Throughout these pages I reflect on ways to build up

our self-acceptance and self-love, because our relationship to ourselves, more than anything else, informs how we show up in the world: what we think, what we say, and what we do. Our relationship to ourselves serves as the foundation for more *or less* meaning, connection, and joy in our lives. Let's aim for more of all these things, because why wouldn't we?

I've separated this book into three parts: YOU, ME, and US. In the YOU section, there's a good deal of cheerleading, like *Hey, you're worthy and you can do it and you're some kind of warrior or you'd never have gotten this far!* In here I have fun with the promise of the book's title — that you are, without question, enough as you are. You'll want to stay in this section if you need a little lift, a pep talk, a reminder that you're not just human but divine, that the energy that created the mountains and stars is the same energy flowing through you right now and always. And that's a very good thing.

In the ME section, there's a bit more self-reflection and personal responsibility. I write about some of the more challenging aspects of being human, like, among other things, being an envious monster, a sensitive neurotic, and a sometimes asshole. Well, and a profoundly loving man, of course, who recognizes his power whenever he chooses kindness, empathy, and compassion. You'll want to chill in this section when you need to be reminded that everything about you is human and okay — and yes, I'm referring to those uncomfortable nasty bits too. Hear this, please: Nothing within you lives outside the bounds of love. Seriously, *nada*. And that too is a very good thing.

The US section often feels like a call to action, like *Come on, y'all, let's be brave and vulnerable and own our shit and make this world a better place for us all.* It's kind of a blend of the YOU and ME sections, personal and collective responsibility with some hearty cheerleading. You'll want to camp in this section when it's time to remember how powerful we are in pairs, teams, or as a community to awaken this world with honesty and love and transform our reality because of it. Truly, there are no limits to the power of people united in love.

In my last book, *Big Love*, I focused on past experiences and the lessons I gleaned from them, in order to guide us into more love-centered choices right now. This book, however, lives in the present, in the understanding that it's what we do from this moment on that matters the most, no matter what we've done or what's been done to us up until this point. Really take that in for a second: *It's what you do from this moment on that matters the most.* What a liberating truth. And it will forever be the case, because we continue to be given new moments each second of every day.

Since there's always a new now, it's never too late to strengthen the relationship you have with yourself, to accept the whole of you, even what you see as your unlikable parts, and to grow more in love with yourself all the time. For real. Self-love is a skill, and as with all skills, the more you practice at it, the better you become. It's the only possibility. By deepening your love for yourself, you naturally deepen the love you have for others as well, and for our planet. With love as a guiding force, all is possible, all the time. Yet another very good thing.

I'll leave you here, dear reader, with sincere hope that this book encourages you to commit to loving yourself, no matter what. And in so doing, may you never forget your radiant humanity and transcendent divinity.

Remember always:

> You
> are
> whole
> beautiful
> wild
> strong
> gifted
> worthy
> sacred
> loved
> and enough,
> as you are.

Thank you for being here.

YOU

Either
all the
people
who love you
are totally misguided
or you're extremely lovable.

Every ounce of energy you put into being some-one you are not takes away from the indescribable joy that comes with being yourself. When you're brave enough to live in your truth — quirks, insecurities, fears, and all — you carve out paths for others to do so as well. You inspire in them the same commitment to a life without falseness, a deep desire for something real. You are everything you need to be, and what a gift you give our world by being yourself.

Do not limit yourself because of past realities. Who you are right now is someone you have never been before, with more experience and insight than you've ever had. Be willing to believe in yourself. Be willing to trust yourself. You can manifest life-changing wonders when you believe in your ability to create them.

How others see you doesn't represent the truth of who you are, but only their perception of you. Nothing more. And that will always be beyond your control, so don't own what others think of you. That's for them to own. Your job, should you choose it, is to work at loving yourself, and accepting yourself, as much as you are able. That includes your crooked smile and atypical fashion sense and bizarre family history and even your penchant for garden gnomes. Look, you like what you like. There will only ever be one you, just one in all of eternity. Whatever it is that makes you *you* can be something to celebrate, if you let it, instead of something to feel ashamed of or less than on account of. You are beautiful, and enough, just as you are. Really, just as you are.

Every single
thing within you
is worthy of love.
Even better,
you have the power
to love every single
thing within you.
Invite it all in
to your heart,
welcome it all home,
and let your love
make friends
with the whole of you.

Not one thing
you have done
in your entire life
lives outside the
bounds of forgiveness.
It's time to forgive yourself.
For everything. All of it.

You never know when you'll be the person who ignites an awakening in someone else. That's why it's so important to weave kindness and love into our interactions as often as possible. It may be in the advice you give your dearest friend or the unfiltered smile you offer to some stranger at the store. It may be your willingness to stop whatever it is you're doing to listen or the way in which you allow your eyes to rest on another without judgment. You can't predict when you will be the catalyst for something wonderful to light up another human being, but there will be many such moments when your love and compassion are just what someone needs to feel understood, and okay, and inspired. To feel seen.

Don't forget
to surrender
to the moments
of joy that
present themselves.
Immerse yourself
in every wave
of bliss that dares
to swallow you.
Soften. Sink.
Let yourself go.

Just show up, as you are. You don't have to look or feel great. You don't have to be prepared for each challenge or know all the hows of every situation. You don't have to be fearless, have all the answers, or be 100 percent ready. Nobody is any of these things. Nobody ever was. It's not about being perfect at all. You just have to show up, as you are, despite all the objections and insecurities of your mind, despite each and every fear that threatens to hold you back, despite the limitations and criticisms others will place on you. To hell with all that. This is your life, your journey, your adventure, and all it's asking of you is to show up for it, as you are. That's enough. That's more than enough. That's everything.

The norm
is no place
for a
Beautiful
Freak
like you.

Stare at the trees,
smell the trees,
touch the trees,
and listen - yes, listen -
with your whole body
and soul to the trees.
Get close to the trees
and closer still, and
become the most
treelike human you can be.

It's okay
to numb
yourself -
with food
or booze,
drugs or sex,
shopping or
the internet,
or all of them
in the same hour -
because this
reality is hard
as hell to live in,
with, and through.
And when you're
done numbing,
let yourself feel
again, because
deeper than
that need to
numb your life
is the need
to feel your life.

Try not
to cling
to stories
about
yourself
that are no
longer true,
or to ones
that never
were in the
first place.

Some people will judge you, no matter what you do. Whether you choose to live in the box of societal conditioning or in the freest expression of your authenticity, you will be judged. Knowing this, why continue to choose the box? If people are going to judge you anyway, let them judge you for your truth.

Let the violence and pain in our world root you even more deeply in your commitment to be kinder and love harder, no matter the person or circumstance. Your great ability to love has everything to do with creating a more peaceful reality on our planet. Your love matters. It makes a critical difference. It helps us all.

And then there was that time
you sucked down your fear,
breathed into it, faced it with
a courage that could move mountains,
and you stepped right into
the truth, the situation, the experience
that moments (and forever) before
had crippled and controlled you
and had you believing
you could never rise up to meet it.
But you did, because you could,
and you will again, because you can.
Yes, you can.

Quit putting off the conversations you know you need to have. Say what you need to say, with as much honesty, clarity, and love as possible. And really listen in return, with empathy and compassion. Yes, it's scary to speak the fullness of your truth, and hard to hear the whole truth of another, but there's no real way to move a relationship forward without the courage to express yourself honestly. And yes, *forward* may mean going your separate ways. If that's where an honest conversation leads, then it can only be good for both of you.

Don't waste
your time
explaining
yourself
to those
determined to
misunderstand you.

There's
nothing
to fix
about you.
Only things
to remember.

Some people will not jibe with who you are and what you have to say. Some will misunderstand you, while others may understand you perfectly well and simply not like you, for whatever reason. All of this has nothing to do with you, not really. You can't control how others respond to you.

Try not to limit yourself, your authentic expression, out of fear of being judged or criticized or made fun of. We are judged, criticized, and made fun of by some no matter how we choose to show up. That's one of the less fun parts of being human.

And yes, it's true that if you keep quiet, blend in, or hide yourself, you won't attract as much attention or judgment from others. (People are more comfortable with those who stay silent.) But — and this is a big *but* — when you hide yourself behind your fears and live in a whisper when you were born to sing, you don't invite the same beautiful connections and possibilities that come with living your life out loud. Not fearless, but brave just the same. So committed to being yourself that you forget how to be anyone else. More than anything, free.

What you behold
as beautiful
is a reflection
of the beauty
within you.
You cannot see
what you are not.
To lose yourself
in the radiance
of a golden sunset
is to find inside yourself
a light no less luminous
than any miraculous sky,
no less incandescent
than a thousand blazing fires.

There is room for you in this world – for your creativity, opinions, and desires; for your sadness, laughter, and fears. There is room for everything you have to offer. Really. Every single thing. You can't be too big, too brave, too outrageous. You can't give or express too much, feel or release too much. If you can learn to accept your whole self, it matters little whether others can. There is room for you here, an invitation to be the full realization of yourself, to leap into the beauty of your becoming, to let your entirety unfold. You are beautiful. You are worthy. You are enough. Feel it. Believe it. Declare it. There will always be room for you here.

It's not the pain
but your ability
to be with the pain
that changes,
that shifts over time.
You grow larger
than what debilitates,
until the mighty boulder
crushing your heart
becomes a single stone
resting upon your chest.
The pain remains, real
and even heavy at times,
but no longer suffocating,
no longer the only story.
You have expanded too far
(a universe all your own)
to stay oppressed by its weight.

Try loving
that part
of yourself
that is unable
to love all the
parts of yourself.

You get to a point when you just don't want to be pushed anymore. Pushed to pretend you're okay with condescending behavior and disrespectful attitudes. Pushed to ignore the determined yearnings of your clearest truth. Pushed to engage in conversations and situations that in no way serve your peace or joy. Pushed to act a bogus part and clap for those who are acting theirs. Pushed to be quiet and stay small, to exist rather than live. You get to a point when it's all too much, too exhausting, too false. Something must change. Then you realize the changes you crave have always been within your power to create. You realize no one has the might to push you into anything when you are unwilling to budge. You realize that you, more effectively than any outside influence, have been your biggest pusher all along. So you stop — stop pushing and pretending and shrinking. You stop it all, because you can. Because you must. And you don't waste much time regretting that you didn't do it sooner. You're suddenly much too busy living your free and vital life for such silly regrets.

I see you.
I see your strength and courage,
your hesitations and fears.
I see the way you love others
and your struggle to love yourself.
I see how hard you work to grow
and your dedication to heal.
I see your vulnerable humanity
and your transcendent divinity.
You are beautiful, my friend,
and so very worthy, just as you are.
I see you, and I love what I see.

Become
so wild
the world
gives up
on trying
to tame you.

Not everyone will be able to handle your truth. Some will condemn you, and that's okay. People fear what they don't understand. But there's a sweet flip side. A balance. Some will be so inspired by your courage, by your willingness to be yourself, that they'll begin to open up to a truth inside themselves they didn't know was there. Or did know but were too scared to acknowledge. They will start to dance into their freedom, groove into all that makes them unique. And you will have been the spark to their light, because you were strong enough, brave enough to ignite your own. Your happiness is reason enough to be yourself, but if you need another, think of the others, think of our world of followers needing someone to lead. Needing to lead themselves. Home.

Don't make any big decisions
when you're feeling angry,
misunderstood, or resentful.
Allow yourself to process,
to return to some version
of peace, and then decide
what you need to do from there.

Change.
Or don't.
Either way,
be willing
to love yourself.

You can't
paint your
self-portrait
with someone
else's hand.

If you had been ready to leave that unhealthy relationship sooner, you would have. The same goes for that miserable job, or the spiritual community that stopped feeling like home, or the addictive habit you couldn't quite kick. You weren't ready to walk away until you walked away. Why continue to beat yourself up for not having done it sooner? Sooner couldn't have been the right time, or you would have moved on then. There's no point in abusing yourself for having stayed in a difficult situation much longer than you would have preferred. What's done is done. You move forward when you're ready. And when you're ready and move forward, it can't be too late. It can only be the right time.

Find people who can handle your darkest truths, who don't change the subject when you share your pain or try to make you feel bad for feeling bad. Find people who understand we all struggle, some of us more than others, and that there's no weakness in admitting it. In fact, few things take as much strength. Find people who want to be real, however that looks and feels, and who want you to be real too. Find people who get that life is hard, and who get that life is also beautiful, and who aren't afraid to honor both of those realities. Find people who help you feel more at home in your heart, mind, and body, and who take joy in your joy. Find people who love you, for real, and who accept you, for real. Just as you are. They're out there, these people. Your chosen family is waiting for you. Don't stop searching until you find them.

Your truth
is in no way
rooted in
the opinions
of others,
so don't let
the opinions
of others
uproot you
from your truth.
Stand strong
in who you are,
free and undeniable,
and let the singular
light you cast
be colored
with authenticity.

"

Not everything
is about you.
In fact, most
things aren't.
What a **relief, right?**

There are any number of reasons why a person may not be making time for you, but they all fall under the umbrella of them not making time for you. If that's making you sad or frustrated, maybe it's time to acknowledge you're continuing to hope for or expect something that isn't happening. And may never happen. Maybe it's best to put your energy somewhere else, at the very least into people who reciprocate your level of interest and not only get excited by the prospect of hanging out with you but actually make the time to do it.

When you live authentically, you will not always meet the expectations of others. That's okay. Let them come to expect someone different, someone un-bound. Let them come to expect your fierce commitment to being real. Let them come to expect your inability to compromise yourself for the benefit of those who are more comfortable when you stay quiet and play small. You don't need to change yourself to meet the world's expectations. The world will figure out a way to accept and love you as you are. Or not. Either way, you're free.

There are
so many people
to love in our world.
Still, begin with yourself.

Maybe all that discomfort is just wall after wall breaking down, years and a lifetime of conditioning that can no longer stand alongside your authentic expression. So the walls crumble, and it hurts. And it's necessary. Every path to freedom travels through so much pain, though it's always worth it as you discover your courage, keep taking steps forward, and eventually remember what it feels like to be free.

There's a time to compromise
and a time to say no more.
Doing either from an honest place
feels exactly the same: like freedom.

I'm a fan of stillness, of deep breaths, of sinking into the silence of things. But sometimes you have to make noise for your life. You have to get fired up, stomp around, and let Spirit know you're here and amped and ready to do whatever it takes to heal and grow. You have to show up in your story. Be present, willing, and committed. Active, feisty, and intentional. Let life know you're ready to create change and to love yourself like never before, and nothing will keep you from realizing your most beautiful life. And then meditate some, because, well, balance is key.

Be
a spot
of color
in other
people's gray.

Let them judge you.
Let them misunderstand you.
Let them gossip about you.
Their opinions aren't your problem.
You stay kind, committed to love,
and free in your authenticity.
No matter what they do or say,
don't you dare doubt your worth
or the beauty of your truth.
Just keep on shining like you do.

Don't
cage
others
because
you're
afraid
to fly.

You are not obligated to give energy to self-abusive thoughts. The moment you become aware of them, do your best to focus your mind on something else, like your favorite sweater or a pretty tree or that chubby squirrel that keeps hiding nuts in your yard. If thinking about yourself makes you feel like crap, then stop thinking about yourself for now. There's a world of beauty and weirdness to consider without needing to beat yourself up. You can return to thoughts about yourself when you've got nicer things to think. Maybe start with some general niceties, like the fact that you're a kind person most of the time, a good friend to your loved ones, and, if you're honest, pretty funny in your own way. You get to choose where your energy goes, so give energy to thoughts like these. Starve self-hatred and it dies. Feed it and it thrives. The same goes for self-love. Feed it. Let it grow and expand and thrive. Commit to raising your self-love the way you would your precious child: Tend to it with utter devotion, and decide there's not one thing more important to you in the entire world. Let self-love, not self-abuse, be your obligation. And see how every single thing in your life begins to change.

Forgive
the minds
of the world.
They will
never
be able
to grasp
your beauty.
You've been
designed
to thrill the hearts.

Of course change is hard. It has to be. It carries with it, every single time, the potential to elevate, even revolutionize, your life in ways you can never truly realize until you're already transformed, safely on the other side of your resistance and fear. Change is hard, yes, but it's rarely as difficult as not doing anything when you know in your bones you need to make a change.

There
will
never
be a
single
reason
to
give
up on
yourself,
so don't
even
think
about it.

First,
tell
yourself
the truth.
Start there.
Be willing to
love yourself
no matter what
you discover,
and then see
what unfolds.

It's 100 percent okay not to have a clue what you want to do with your life. There's so much pressure to find your passion and know your destiny and realize your calling…*and please leave me alone I can't even figure out what I want for breakfast.* It's okay to not know what you want to do. Or who you want to be. Or where you want to live, or with whom. So much of life is not knowing. Discovering. Playing. It's okay to want to know too. Curiosity is a great place to start. Follow it and see where it takes you. Ask yourself deeper questions. Instead of *What should I do with my life?* try *What things add meaning to my life?* or *What feels good and makes me smile?* When you ask more specific questions, you get more specific answers, clearer stepping stones on the path to who knows what. But don't beat yourself up for not knowing. It's not a race. And it's not like you can miss your destiny. You're living it every moment of every day. It's yours, only yours, ever unfolding. The boredom, the pressure, each moment of joy, and everything else all play a part in your becoming.

When someone rejects you, for whatever reason, that rejection reflects their wants, not your limitations. You are in no way defined by the rejection, or the acceptance, of anyone else. Your worth depends on no one.

Maybe what you're holding on to isn't really about the other person at all. Maybe it's about you not wanting to let go of something that's been around for so long, not wanting to part with a connection that's been comfortable enough, even if it no longer is. Maybe you'll find even greater comfort in the letting go, in the belief that you are worthy of more than they could offer, and more than you together were able to create.

You will
not once
regret
choosing
to ignore
your
mind's
abuse
and deciding
instead
to accept
and love yourself
exactly as you are.

The more you fight against your circumstances, the harder you'll struggle to move beyond them. Wars create wars, internally and externally. Accept your circumstances completely. Breathe into the reality of your life. Own it for what it is. Then, from this place of acceptance, from the peaceful acknowledgment that, if you want to, you can transform what is into something different and wonderful, begin to take the necessary steps to change your life.

People can't
read your mind,
not even those
closest to you.
No matter
how sensitive
you think
someone is
or should be,
they can't
always know
what you need or
how you're feeling
unless you tell them.
It's up to you
to communicate
what's going on with you.

Why spend your time fighting to make a damaging reality work? Be willing to move on from the people and situations that don't serve your heart. You are capable of creating and sustaining relationships rooted in respect, equality, and love. You just have to believe you are worthy of them. And of course you are worthy of them.

There will always be reasons you're not ready enough and always fears that will beg you not to follow your heart's calling. Sometimes the only way to overcome all the obstacles your mind presents is to start wherever you are with whatever you have to offer in the moment. To trust that this is enough and that you're enough. Really, just begin.

Maybe your
mind's plan
needs your
heart's revision.

Sure, wings are fun,
but the only thing you
really need to fly is
a heart bold enough
to love everything
in its path, and a mind
open enough to let
the heart do its thing.

Be
willing
to go
the distance
for yourself.
You are
worthy of
your everything.

When you can (as soon as possible), stand in front of a mirror, gaze into your eyes, and say to the magnificent person standing before you, *I believe in you*. If those words don't feel honest, try, *I am willing to believe in you* or *I am committed to believing in you*, and see if that feels better. Give yourself over to these words. There will never be a person whose belief matters more to you than yourself, and it's never too late to foster that belief with willingness, intention, and commitment. Your biggest cheerleader is already alive within you, a heart bursting with love and belief in who you are and what you have to offer. You simply need to stop drowning out the cheers, open yourself to your heart, and listen.

You are
some kind
of warrior
or you'd
never have
gotten this far.

No one but you can fulfill your dreams, so don't let others discourage you from pursuing them. Most are terrified of change and failure and often aren't ready to support another person's courage when they're not able to make brave choices for themselves. It's easier for some people to congratulate you once you're on the other side of your goal than to cheer you on while you struggle through the pursuit of it. Don't wait for cheerleaders. You may not get them. Just keep doing what you feel in your heart you need to do. Take one step, and then another. You'll get where you need to be.

Before you put yourself down, please consider all you've accomplished to get to this point, every life you've touched and each time you've moved forward beyond your fears. Please consider how truly kick-ass you are and that our world is a much more beautiful place with you in it. Don't waste your energy tearing yourself down, not when there are so many reasons to build yourself up. You are worthy of nothing less than the deepest love and appreciation you have to share. Share it with yourself. Today and every day. For real, you're an inspiration.

Trust yourself,
and when you can't,
trust your life,
and when you can't,
trust your God,
and when you can't,
trust your inability
to trust anything
for the moment.

I wish
you knew
how normal
your feelings are,
and how universal
your struggle is.
You are so not alone,
dear one. You couldn't
be alone if you tried.

If you make one commitment, let it be to love yourself as wildly as possible. No exceptions. No conditions. No restraint.

Repeat these words:

I commit to loving myself with everything I've got, even when I'm inclined not to, even when my mind directs me otherwise, even when others treat me poorly, even when I'm exhausted and overwhelmed and feel like I have nothing more to give. Even then, I will give my love to myself, because I am important, and worthy, and divine. I will love myself wholly, wildly, and without inhibition because I understand that by doing so I open my entire world to choices, connections, and realities rooted in this love I give to myself. By loving myself, I invite love into every aspect of my life, as well as the lives of everyone I encounter. I commit to loving myself because I am a being of love and function at my beautiful best when I live in, from, and with this astounding wealth of love I have to share. For these reasons, and for every other life-affirming reason that exists in this world, I hereby commit to loving myself with absolutely everything I've got.

You are worth this pledge to yourself. It will change everything.

What a
fucking
Beauty
you are.
For real.

ME

I am becoming more
relaxed with who I am,
and more gentle with
myself when I'm not able
to be relaxed with who I am.
I am committed to this gentleness.
With it, I remind myself
I am human, and even when
I disappoint myself, or others,
I am worthy and I am loved.

I look around and see so much fear, people getting more and more comfortable with their hate, more at ease being mean, more united in their division. And I think, *No. Not me. I will not get lost in this fearful world. I will not play with bullies. I will continue to be brave and kind. I will speak for empathy and compassion. And no matter what, I will never stop loving.*

It's so
strange
to not know
how I feel
sometimes,
unable to
decide if
I'm pretty
peaceful
or maybe
going insane.

Living with intention doesn't mean everything falls into place exactly as I intend it to (though it improves the odds, for sure). It means I believe that everything is energy and that my life is important enough to consciously consider my choices. It means that being intentional feels a lot better, and stands to create more exciting outcomes, than drifting through my days on autopilot.

"
It frustrates me to feel
so insecure much of the time.
It exhilarates me to be
courageous despite my insecurities.

There is a voice in my mind that insists I'm not enough. I don't believe this voice, but I love it still. There is a story I've carried that says I'm not worthy of love. I know this story is a lie, and I love it still. There is shame within that tells me I'm inherently flawed. I'm certain that's false, but I choose to love it still. I no longer believe many of my thoughts, and definitely not those working hard to tear me down. I no longer desire to go to war with them, either. These thoughts don't define me, but they are a part of my mind and therefore of me, and I am committed to loving all of me, not just the easy parts. Whether or not I like it, I will love it still.

What I'm willing to allow in my life directly relates to how I feel about myself, which is why self-love is a critical component of any peaceful life. When I feel I'm not enough, I allow for relationships and circumstances that mirror this feeling. When I connect to the truth of my worthiness, I invite relationships and situations that honor my worth and am no longer as likely to give my time and energy to ones that don't. My worth won't allow it. It all begins with self-love, with understanding the power we have to transform our lives by creating a loving and accepting relationship with ourselves. Again and again, I have enhanced my life with a deeper dedication to loving myself. Again and again, I have created more peace and joy by resting in the truth that I am worthy and enough, exactly as I am. Exactly as I am. As are you.

Everywhere I look I see people doing their best to make sense of this overwhelming reality, and to be kind, authentic human beings despite the many invitations we all receive to be phony, unkind assholes. Sometimes their best doesn't look like much to me, and I remind myself that my best doesn't look like much a lot of the time, either. I empathize. I recognize their humanity as I do my own. We're all human, and we're all struggling to some degree. Every single one of us, every single day. In this knowing, I connect to compassion, to love, and to the acceptance that it's not my job to police the paths of others, not when it takes so much effort to light my own way.

I focus on being
as present as possible
with what's before me,
no matter what that is,
and on accepting it's often
difficult for me to be wholly
present with what's before me.
I aim to stop trying so hard
to be here now because the now
often gets lost in the trying.

The moments when I feel most peaceful with this world's insanity and the wild aggression of my mind are the moments when I remember I'm a child of God, with the energy of Spirit running through me, bold and boundless and always beckoning love. Source energy, the creator of all things, fills my blood and bones and every breath I take. It just takes remembering this forever connection to the Divine for me to be able to breathe more deeply, to love with complete devotion, and to give myself another moment of peace in a warring world. Whatever it is we call this holy energy, this limitless creative spirit, it feeds us all, if we let it — if we let ourselves become one with it, and then by extension one with ourselves, and then, naturally, one with each other.

My jealousy tells me that if I'm not chosen it's because I'm not enough, there's something wrong with me, I will always be less than. My jealousy comes to life in my gut, burns circles through my chest, makes it impossible to eat and hard to breathe. It hurts, and then hurts more, and because it allows no other thought, begins to kill. My jealousy seeks to destroy me.

But sometimes I remember to engage with my jealousy, though not as prey, and not in war. When its poison infects me I get curious. I listen to it, let it tear me down and turn friends into enemies. I see how it hurts my body, how it makes me want to hurt others, how it never stops trying to kill.

And then I exit my mind, jealousy's creator, poison maker, destroyer of self. I enter my heart for a different opinion. And it offers one, simple and clear. *No matter what*, it tells me, *you are enough. There is no other possibility. You are worthy too. And you are loved, deeply loved, whether or not you are chosen, whether or not you are seen. So,* my heart asks, *are you ready to believe me? Are you ready to be free — of your jealousy, and your blame, and your deep self-loathing?*

I am, I say, *but I don't know how.*

Ah, but you do, it says. *You're doing it right now, just by being here. Stay with me, and I'll teach you to love it all, even the jealousy that wants to kill you, even the mind that will never let you be. Stay with me,* my heart implores, *and I'll teach you to be free.*

I've got you,
my body told me,
and I will heal what I can.
But for you to be healthy, it said,
you must learn to feel what you can.

I'm taking
a break
from what is
to spend
more time
with what can be.

I am here
to give myself
over to love,
again and again,
no matter what.
It's that simple,
and that difficult.

You know what I love
as much as having
a wildly productive day?
Having a wildly unproductive day
and not judging myself for it.
Doing a whole lot of nothing
and loving myself just the same.

I don't expect my neuroses to disappear, but they don't carry the same weight as they once did because I don't feel as heavy about them. I don't judge my perfectionism, obsessive thinking, envy, and compulsive habits the way I used to. I see them as part of being human, and I've chosen to accept them as aspects of my personality. I find them annoying, even crippling at times, but I try not to begrudge myself for them. I don't believe we evolve out of our personalities as much as we evolve into a more expansive acceptance of who we are. I'm learning to let my mind be without the compulsion to become my mind. In my commitment to love myself, I shower love on the frustrating bits too. I become the sky and don't fret as much about my inclement weather.

In the course of one day, even one hour, I can waver between feeling deeply connected to the work I'm doing and the why behind it, and feeling like I have no idea why I'm here and what the point of anything is anyway. It's hard to look at a world that seems to be imploding in countless ways and feel connected to any clear purpose within the implosion. I find my mind asking, *What's the point?* a lot of the time. What I come back to, when I'm not lost in terror and hopelessness, is the same thing I always come back to in my clarity: just love. That's the point, at least for me, at least in this lifetime. Whether I see the world as deteriorating or flourishing, the point is to offer it my love. Offer myself and others my love. Every single time I center back in love, it awakens something within me. It brings me back to myself. It carries me home.

"

I survived
as still water
contained by
my surroundings,
then flowed
as a river
and began
carving my
own path.

When I'm feeling envious, as I often do, because my mind steeps itself in insecurity, competition, and the lie of scarcity, I remind myself that to envy is human, that I am not a bad person because I have ugly thoughts about another's successes, and that even though my mind is trying to convince me otherwise, I am enough, as I am, no matter what I do or don't do moving forward. Once I get grounded, or at least am no longer spinning out as much, I explore what exactly it is I am envying. Where might there be a deeper call within me to give energy to some aspect of my life I've been neglecting? How might this person I envy serve as inspiration? Throughout this process, when I'm able to do so honestly, I rest in my heart and pray for their continued success, or joy, or whatever it is they're experiencing that has triggered my own fears and insecurities. I doubt I'll ever like this envious aspect of my personality, but I am committed to hearing rather than denying it, and loving it and myself still.

I looked at my life
and for the first time
felt like I could hold it all.
That I didn't need
to let go of anything
in order to be whole.
That even those things
I'd been clinging to
had a place in my freedom.
That every single thing played its role.

And then
my sorrow
whispered to me,

I am not here to crush you.
I have not come for your hope.

I only want you to feel
the deep pain of this world
so you will love everyone
in it that much more.

Then my
heart opened
wider than it
ever had before,
and all I saw
before me,
everywhere
I looked,
were people to love.

I **know that** when I haven't found forgiveness, I'm operating from my mind and not my heart, from fear and not love. Which means I have more work to do, more truth to uncover. I understand that my inability to forgive means I'm lost in the hopelessness of the past rather than the possibility of the present, a disciple of blame rather than a master of acceptance. When I continue to blame others for their past actions — no matter how hurtful — and how those actions still affect me today, I hand over the power of responsibility for my life. I give someone else control. When I root myself in the present moment, no longer a victim of my painful past, I take ownership of my reality and eliminate the possibility of blame. There is no place for blame in forgiveness, and no path to forgiveness through blame. If blame were the path, I suspect we'd all be master forgivers.

I **was a victim,** until I decided I wasn't. Until I realized only I had the final say in my victimhood. That it was a choice. My choice. Before then, I allowed the actions of others to define me. I allowed painful, unfair circumstances to dictate how I announced myself to the world. I gave up control of who I was and who I wanted to be, at home — but lost — in a victim's life. So I made the choice to find myself. I couldn't take responsibility for everything that happened to me. Bad things happen to us all, even when we don't invite them. But I could own my response to all of it. Everything. The moment I chose to do so, I ignited a strength I'd long forgotten and saw, at last, new possibilities for my life. I opened the door to deeper healing and to endless opportunities for real change. The very moment I chose to take responsibility for my life, I acknowledged my power like never before. And I have never again been a victim.

I had to learn
to see my shadow
and hold my pain
in its fullness,
with acceptance
and forgiveness,
so that I could
release the hate
I felt for myself
and quit hurling it
blindly at others.

Often the only comfort I can find in despair is the understanding that it, like everything else, won't last forever. I tell myself to wait it out, to cry and scream and do whatever it takes to feel. Or if feeling is too much, and sometimes it is, then I eat ice cream and watch TV and sleep. Yes, keep sleeping. *Nothing lasts forever, I remind myself. Nothing has, and nothing will. Just wait it out, until the sorrow starts to crack, and the smallest glint of hope peeks through, expanding ever so steadily into something that resembles light.* Yes, light. A light that reflects a life beyond despair.

Even though I don't define success in terms of money, power, and popularity, I see how my mind still gets lost in those false notions of what it means to be successful. My ego wants more cash, more cachet, and more clicks. There can't ever be enough of any of them. That's not success, of course. That's conditioning. Addiction. Desperation.

Love invites me to see success differently, as the fullest embodiment of kindness and compassion I'm capable of expressing. When I'm loving, I'm successful. When I'm forgiving, I'm successful too. I've come to view success through a lens of humanity, and the degree to which I'm successful directly aligns with the degree to which I love myself and my fellow human beings. This definition of success fires me up and keeps me striving for more.

In this moment
I am grateful for
all the love that
has touched my life,
and for all the lives
I have touched
with my love.

And then it hit me:
I don't have to participate
in these toxic conversations.
But if I choose to,
I can set a different example.
I can bring love to the moment,
regardless of the response,
and choose to be kind,
to empathize, no matter what.
I can root myself
in our shared humanity
and remind myself:
My power lives in love.

The less fixed I become in the stories I've created about my personality, the more I learn about and surprise myself. It's no longer *never* or *always*, because there are few things I would never or always do. I've learned this about myself by making choices I thought I never would, and by parting with ones I expected to make forever.

I don't expect to transcend all my conditioning around beauty. I accept I may never be able to look in the mirror and like all I see. And that's okay. Not ideal, but okay. I can, however, be gentle with myself, no matter how I view my looks and body. I can remove the expectation to be more evolved when I see my reflection, and bring acceptance and grace to however I feel. Self-love means more than finding myself physically beautiful, which can be wildly difficult for most of us. Self-love invites me to be kind to myself, no matter how much I like or don't like what I see in the mirror. Self-love reminds me, in my inability to transcend a lifetime of conditioning around appearance, that it's okay, that I'm human.

I will not
let my shame
keep me from
telling the truth.

Hate is a destroyer. Love is a healer. When we look at our world and ourselves, we know this to be true. I refuse to be someone who hates anyone. I refuse to be led by impulses to dehumanize others, no matter how horrible I believe their actions to be. It's not helpful. I will give myself over to love, no matter what, because I long for a world that does the same, and I know any hatred I ignite within only fuels the hatred I see outside. There's just no way to hate ourselves or each other into a loving world.

When
I'm paying
attention,
and honest,
I see that
there really
isn't anything
I judge
in others
that isn't
alive in me
to some degree.

I cherish the friends
who are willing
to let me know
when I'm acting
like an asshole
and who know how
to do so with love.

I **felt like doing my part** to change the world, so I started by giving thanks for all the blessings in my life, rather than bemoaning all that was missing from it. Then I complimented my reflection in the mirror, instead of criticizing it as I usually did. Next I walked into my neighborhood and offered kindness to everyone I passed, whether or not they offered theirs to me. Each day I did these things, and soon they became habit. Each day I lived with more gratitude, more self-love, and more kindness. And sure enough, the world around me began to change. Because I had decided so, I was single-handedly doing my part to change it.

I'm super fucking sensitive. I love this about myself only slightly more than I can't stand it. Sometimes I wish I were an unfeeling stone who didn't take everything so personally and didn't need so much space all the time. Feeling can get exhausting fast. Mostly, though, I know my sensitivity is a superpower, perhaps my greatest, and it's the thing that keeps me loving our world in a profound way. When I'm not too busy hiding from it, that is.

As much as I love
to see the sun set
behind a city skyline,
and feel the pure majesty
of a wild river, and fade,
then disappear, into a
transcendent book or song,
I am always most astounded,
moved, and transported
by the warmth and kindness
of a loving human being. Always.

Along with being joyful, let me be okay with my sadness. As well as belonging, let me be at peace with my loneliness. Let me cradle my anger with the same acceptance I bring to my compassion, and hold space for my insecurity as I do for the belief in myself. Being human isn't easy a lot of the time, but I see how much harder I make it by resisting my complete humanity, by welcoming what's easy to accept about myself while avoiding what's difficult to own. I am no longer interested in rejecting any part of myself. All aspects of who I am are welcome here, and none will any longer be received with shame. To all of myself I will say, again and again, *I love you. You have a home here always. I love you.*

Please
don't mistake
my commitment
to being a kind
and loving person
as any sort
of willingness
to put up
with bullshit.

I have learned
(mostly)
not to go to war
with my mind
but have too often
forgotten to love it.
Why stop with
a peace treaty
when real friendship
is a possibility?
Why stop with tolerance
when there can be love?

Just as I was about to spite my darkness, I considered how strong I'd grown in its shadows, how resilient I'd become from its tests, and how compassionate I now was to other people's pain. I understood that my darkness, as cruel and unbearable as it was sometimes, never stopped contributing to all that made me whole. So I closed my eyes and whispered a thank-you to the darkness, and to the light, and to every single thing that has played a hand in my being here at all.

I **don't judge falseness** the way I used to, but I can't stomach it the way I used to, either. I'm working too hard to be honest and real, to be who I am. It's strange to have to work at being who you are. No other animal has this struggle. And yet we live in a world that celebrates conformity, and my mind wants me to conform. *Don't be too honest*, it tells me. And sometimes I'm not. *Don't show that part of yourself*, it warns. And sometimes I don't. Other times I'm just the right amount of honest and show exactly what I feel like showing. Those times feel scary and exciting and represent not just who I want to be but who I am. I have trouble stomaching falseness in others because I can't bear it in myself. Pretending is only fun when it's understood as an act, not when it's used to mask something true. Lies don't get us anywhere good, but damn, are we all good liars. I don't judge falseness the way I used to, in myself or others, because we're human and so afraid all the time, of one thing most of all — the one thing that could set us free: simply being who we are here to be.

A person's humanity is always
there on some level. Always.
If I can't find it, I know it's time
to search a little harder for my own.

Love reminds me I have nothing to be ashamed of and therefore don't need to numb myself out of shame. Love encourages me to find forgiveness so that I don't have to escape my anger and blame. Love pushes me to seek connection so that I am no longer compelled to be destructive in my loneliness. Love insists that I am worthy, just as I am, and that I am strong enough to accept and love myself without needing to mask my truth. Every single time I choose love, I'm choosing my health and well-being. And the more I choose love, the more likely I am to create for myself the kind of life I won't need to escape from.

My fear whispered to me,
I am just trying to protect you.
I whispered back,
I know, and I'm stronger than you think.

I may not yet know what I can achieve,
but I've seen what I can overcome,
and I refuse to underestimate myself again.

I used to be so afraid to be with my sadness that I did everything in my power to avoid it. I turned my sadness into a monster that would crush me if I faced it. So I didn't. Only when I started to look at my sadness honestly, to sit in it and feel the pain of it, was I able to see that I could survive it. It wasn't comfortable, but it didn't destroy me; it made me stronger and more compassionate, toward myself and others. I don't fear my sadness like I used to. Or my anger, or my pain. I pay attention to them, I feel them, I stay as open as I can to the lessons they want me to learn. And I take care of and love myself through them. Love matters. It's our greatest healer, after all.

My heart, my inner knowing, my divine align-
ment with Source always nudges me toward love, of self
and others. Always. Toward compassion and forgiveness
and oneness. I have heard people object with some version
of *What if you live in your deepest truth, and your deep-
est truth is telling you to kill someone?* I don't think that's
possible. At our essence I believe we are love. Anything
that compels us against love is not our deepest truth. It's
pain and trauma and fear piled over what is most deeply
true within us. The more I connect to my heart, the more
loving my life becomes. The more I trust my intuition, the
more likely I am to make healthy choices. The more I align
with my soul, the more okay I feel in my being. This is what
I know to be true.

Sometimes
when I feel powerless
I remember how often
I've thought myself into
misery, anxiety, and fear,
and I'm reminded just how
powerful I am when I put
my mighty mind to something.

It's liberating
to acknowledge
my own ignorance
and to let go of
the compulsion
to be right at all costs.
What a gift it is
to be brave enough
to say, *I don't know*,
and braver still
to admit I was wrong.

I have
too often
projected
expectations
onto others
and then
condemned
them for not
becoming
the fictional
characters
I alone
had created.

There are too many reasons to be angry, and I will not live my life in rage. Enraged. Anger is a necessary and powerful emotion when I allow myself to feel it, without becoming it. Without letting it suffocate all the other feelings, without letting it convince me that to be joyful in this time in this world is a crime. Anger is a beautiful catalyst for change, but on its own it can't create healing. Only love can do that. Only that which comes from love can heal. I will not shy away from my anger, or blind myself to the myriad injustices that compel it, but I will continue to remind myself that angry is just one of many ways to feel, and I am here to feel so much more than just angry. And when I am riding the waves of rage, I will continue to invite love in and see what possibilities it is able to create with all my anger.

I see my triggers
as an invitation to look
at the places within myself
that I too condemn,
the places upon which
I need to pour so much
love and acceptance that
my thoughts and feelings
can no longer be dictated
by what anyone else
thinks and feels about me.

My heart
is not too
concerned
with what
makes sense
to my mind,
especially
since what
makes sense
to my mind
often doesn't
make much
sense at all.

To love is to forgive. To forgive is to love. I don't see exceptions, not where my heart is concerned. I don't believe any of the justifications I produce for not forgiving. The only way something could be unforgivable is if I were not loving enough to forgive it, if the darkness that lived within someone's actions proved greater than the light that lives within my heart. I'm not willing to accept that. I won't discount the strength of my love for anything, or anyone.

If only
I could spend
all my days
surrounded
by people
brave enough
to open
their hearts
for real.

I don't wish
for more time.
I wish
for more courage
to live freely
right now.

I **stopped chasing enlightenment** when I finally understood that attaining it was not within my power. Enlightenment is a gift, like winning the spiritual lottery, not an achievement. What is within my power are my kindness, my compassion, and my love. I work on those constantly, and they reward me every day. Their gifts are more than enough for me. If my fate is such that some divine force decides I'm to become enlightened, it won't be because I'm wiser and more peaceful than the rest of the world. I will have just been lucky enough to be born with the winning ticket.

I **get excited by my divinity,** by understanding that the energy that created the oceans and trees and stars is alive within me all the time. Within all of us. Often, however, I need to remember my humanity. My humanness. The fact that I sometimes (often) make choices that aren't the healthiest, that don't serve me in the most beneficial ways. That aren't aligned with my divine nature. I used to beat myself up when I made unhealthy choices. Or when I reacted instead of responded thoughtfully. Or when I didn't achieve what I set out to. Not these days, at least not most of the time. I remind myself I'm only human, and it's okay. I'm okay. I remind myself, as often, that others are only human too. We're all divine, and we're all human. A lot of grace and compassion live in this understanding.

My condemnation
of those who see
differently than I
often highlights
the insecurity I feel
about my point of view.
When I am truly at peace
with my perspective,
I don't need others
to agree with me;
nor do I feel compelled
to condemn those who don't.

I will not give myself over
to the limiting fears of others.
I have my own fears to face,
my own insecurities to accept.
I am not seeking permission anymore
and will no longer stumble
under the weight of doubters
when I was put on this earth to soar.

I seek
to be
more
giving,
and to
remember
I too am
worthy
to receive.

I **keep wanting people** to read my mind and then resenting them a little when they don't. And then I remember we humans aren't mind readers and we're best off just saying whatever it is we need to say, with actual words.

When I'm at peace
with my choices,
I'm far less concerned
with other people's
opinions about them.
When I judge my choices,
I'm much more likely
to internalize
the judgments
of others as well.

Love is always a possibility, and always a healer. Always a possibility, always a healer. When I remember this and ask myself, especially when my mind steeps in self-abuse, *What is love inviting me to do right now?* I am likely to create a bit more peace and acceptance in my being. Not always, but often enough to keep me asking that question.

I **will not set myself up** for a future I don't want by convincing myself it's the future I'm going to get. Neither will I continue to believe that the traumatic events of my past irrevocably determine what's ahead. I will no longer pretend to know what the future holds and won't give energy to predictions of doom when all things are possible.

My mind is
a tricky fucker.
It's the one
with all the
monstrous thoughts
and the one trying
to convince me
I'm the monster.

US

We don't have to
know each other
to love each other.
Let's start by loving
each other and see
what we come
to know from there.

We often take for granted the progress we're making in our lives. Let's stop doing that. Let's acknowledge when we show up with compassion in a situation that typically would have enraged us. Or when we feel some peace instead of the stirring anxiety we're used to feeling. Or when we take the time to offer ourselves love instead of more abuse. These moments matter. They remind us the work we're doing makes a difference and the intentional choices we're making create more peace and meaning in our lives. We are growing and healing precisely because we have committed ourselves to our growth and healing. Because we have decided we are worthy of our love. None of this is an accident. Let's stop treating it as such.

Every petal
plays its part
in the symphony
of our bloom.

"
Compassion
shook its head,
not able to
understand how
so many sufferers,
in a world
full of suffering,
could be so cold
to each other's pain.

When we pray for peace around the world, let's not forget to pray for peace within ourselves. Who will listen to a prayer for peace from those who refuse to model it, from those who lack empathy and compassion, from those always ready for a fight? Peace cannot come from war, and we are all at war with ourselves, and with each other. We have to be willing to confront our own hypocrisies when we pray for peace, to unbury all internal resistance to that call so our prayers will not be muddied by our own unwillingness to rest in love. Where within ourselves are we too aggressors? Where are we unwilling to empathize? Where do we wish for harm to come to those we dislike or don't agree with? Let us become the living examples of the peace we want to see in our world, and then watch how our prayers are magnified, how war cannot endure within the energy of love we together have cocreated. Prayers alone won't do it. We cannot root out war in our world until we root it out in ourselves. Until we return to love.

Our differences are beautiful, and yet sometimes connection requires us to focus on our similarities, like the fact that we all hurt, all struggle, all want to be seen and loved. Maybe if we start there, with this basic understanding of what it means to be alive, we will grow in our connection to one another and learn to love the beautiful differences that embody our improbable human reality.

I'm interested in belonging, but not so much in fitting in. Wanting to fit in feels like a desperate desire of the mind, one that has us contort ourselves away from what's real, into some limited expression of conditioning and expectation. The need to fit in often compels us to deny or lie about who we are and in turn attracts people into our lives who are responding to the false version we've presented. There's very little fulfillment in that. The desire to belong, deep within all of us, offers a different invitation: *Just be yourself*. Then, those we magnetize into our lives can respond to who we are for real. The love and acceptance we feel from these connections tend to be wildly fulfilling, energizing, and true.

Let's follow
the lead
of the sun
and rise
each morning
with the
soul purpose
of shining
our light
on the world.

Life is not easy, and still we make it much harder than it has to be. By ignoring our needs. By staying so busy we don't make time for our needs when we do remember to consider them. By being too afraid to ask others for help, an ear, some attention, or love. By not remembering to give these things to ourselves. Life will never be easy, but with more awareness and intention, it can become less hard.

Love is
the answer.
It has always
been the answer
and will always
be the answer.
We just
have to be
brave enough
to choose it.

I think it's possible to get so in touch with what's true for us, immersed in our innate creativity to such a degree, that to compare ourselves to others would be like comparing ourselves to an elephant, or an oak tree, or a sofa. It simply wouldn't make sense. In our conditioning and fear, we restrict our creativity so it looks like that of others, and then we judge ourselves as less than (sometimes more than) in comparison. In our authenticity, we have gifts, expressions, that are uniquely ours to share. We still see ourselves in others, yes, and them in us, but not in order to limit either, and not in denial of the gifts, the creative impulses, only we have to offer, when we allow for them.

We don't
need to
apologize,
for who
we are
or for who
we are not.

It's one thing to acknowledge how difficult life can be, but it's another to focus on it, to talk about everything that feels wrong all the time, to act like there is only darkness and misery here. In our compulsion not to deny the harsh realities of this unpredictable existence, we often end up denying life's extraordinary beauty. We focus our gaze on division and blind ourselves to real connection; we seek out examples of brutality and ignore the many moments of kindness; we bind ourselves to the opinions of others and silence the deep wisdom of our hearts. In our effort to avoid spiritual bypassing we pass right by the endless exhibits of love on this planet, within this humanity, from one to another and another to one. There is so much hardship — yes, too much — and there is so much beauty too. Where are you looking, and what are you looking for?

Imagine
our world
if we first chose
to learn about
the people
and things
our ignorance
implores us
to condemn.

It's what we do from this moment on that matters the most. It will always be what we do from this moment on that matters the most. We are not bound to any path laid out by past traumas, not when we decide to open ourselves to the endless possibilities that live in each present moment. As long as we are breathing, it can never be too late to change the course of our lives.

Everything we desire is made more likely by seeking it. We don't gift ourselves the radiance of a sunset by hiding indoors, or the thrill of real connection by refusing to see and be seen. We are so powerful in our ability to choose, and act. To create a more fulfilling life demands being active in the creation of it, with belief in our intentions, and trust in the unfolding. A good question to ask ourselves: *What am I seeking, and what am I doing to find it?*

So often we find ourselves unwilling to face a present reality because we know, consciously or subconsciously, we'll also have to face the past. The hardest experiences of our lives never stop living with us. They emerge into our day-to-day existence, and we are left to decide how we want to integrate the pain. Do we build walls to hide it or open doors to face it? Walls have helped me survive when I've needed them, but they've played no part in my healing.

We can't
move on
from that
which we
don't allow
to be.

Self-care necessitates setting boundaries with others. As we grow more adept at taking care of ourselves, we become clearer about our needs and about the things that feel, and don't feel, okay with us. Speak them. If your friend's teasing feels more hurtful than funny, tell her. If you need more alone time in your relationship, let your partner know. Sure, some people may judge your clarity as difficult or unfriendly, but the majority will appreciate knowing what works for you. Most of us don't take joy in overstepping each other's boundaries; we often don't even know we're doing it. We foster healthier, more honest relationships with others, and in turn take better care of ourselves, when we're willing to communicate our boundaries clearly. With clear boundaries, we can bypass the resentment that comes with feeling taken for granted and get down to the important business of loving.

Let's be
much more
expansive
in what
we're able
to visualize
for ourselves
and for
our world.
Let's write
more beautiful,
true, connected
stories.
Let's remember
who we really are,
a wild union of
divinity and humanity,
boundless in our ability
to create, and to love.

A **willingness to forgive** reflects a desire to take care of ourselves. We all know what it feels like to hold on to hatred and blame. It's the worst kind of poison; it clouds everything. By forgiving others, we lift the cloud. Though we may never understand why they did what they did, or in any way condone their actions, or want anything to do with them moving forward, our forgiveness untethers us from the negative bonds of others, and from the victimhood of the pain they caused us. Forgiveness opens the door to a different kind of freedom.

Each of us brings to our experience of another our experience of ourselves. Even the opinions of us that seem entirely personal are influenced by the other's reality and made in great part from a story that has nothing to do with us. A room of one hundred people will have one hundred different experiences of you based on who and where they are in their own lives. I think about this when I'm inclined to take things personally.

It's not a question of courage
(we all have that inside)
but of our willingness to be courageous.

At some point,
if we just
keep moving forward,
the steps begin
to take themselves.

It's **possible to learn** from our mistakes, un-healthy choices, and unkind actions without shaming ourselves in the process. Shame serves nothing and no one. We can be compassionate and gentle with ourselves and still learn, still grow, still evolve into our becoming. There's no such thing as perfection here, in any of us, and no amount of self-abusive behavior will change that. Love is the real game changer, the uplifter, the reminder that we are here to be human, with all that entails, and that we are also, unquestionably, divine.

We need to give ourselves as much support as possible when we're facing our fears or pursuing our dreams or even just struggling to get out of bed and take a shower. Instead of focusing on all the times we failed or fell short, why not focus on all the times we didn't? Why not consider all the different ways we've already done exactly what it is we're trying to do now? We have confronted our fears, we have pushed beyond our comfort zone, we have had difficult conversations, and we have lifted ourselves up after any number of falls. Whatever it is we feel called to do, let's not waste our time convincing ourselves we can't do it. We can do it. We probably already have done it, many times in any number of ways.

Children need to experience more in their lives than adults who love them. They need adults who love themselves too. Kids need self-love modeled for them. They need to understand the critical importance of self-love and be encouraged to develop a relationship with themselves rooted in kindness, compassion, and acceptance. How different, more beautiful, and saner our world would be if children learned that to love themselves, without exception, was the single greatest gift they could give to their lives, their loved ones, and our entire world. And then grew into adults who understood and lived in alignment with this truth.

The sunrise and sunset
are two invitations
every single day
to revel in the beauty
of our world.
Two reminders
to seek beauty
because seeking
will always eventually
lead to finding it,
and every moment
of beauty is a gift
to our hearts, our souls,
our bodies, and
our too-often-weary minds.

When we pay attention to our triggers, our destructive behaviors, and our compulsions, we are likely to discover that many of them are rooted in our childhoods, in the wounds of the children within us who didn't get what they needed from the adults around them. It's never too late to begin healing these wounds, to show up for ourselves as the adults our inner children need. It takes a willingness to get in relationship with the many younger versions of ourselves who felt harmed or neglected and to let them know they are safe, worthy, and loved. To let them shine as they were meant to. And it's not just the little kids within us who need our presence. We need their presence too. Our lives will flourish in new and unpredictable ways once our inner children start showing up for us with their freedom, curiosity, creativity, and joy. Let's comfort and cherish our inner kids and bless ourselves with the gifts they have to share with us, the adults who took the time to be present and love them as they are.

Can we at least acknowledge it's impossible to know how we would react in another person's reality? It's easy to look at someone whose actions we find reprehensible and declare we would never make the same choices. The truth is, we don't know. We haven't lived their life or endured their traumas, and we can't begin to guess the myriad experiences that have led them to say and do what we find so abhorrent. How can we truthfully say that we wouldn't have arrived at the same place if we had walked in their shoes? We can't. Empathy and compassion can be born in this unknowing, if we let them.

We don't
have to
forget
the world
is broken
to give
ourselves
over to fun.
What do you say?
Let's play.

We human beings too often act counter to our innate understandings of life. Our hearts tell us, without exception, to love, and we sicken ourselves daily with hate. Our guts beg us to listen to the wisdom of our bodies, and we instead trust the delusions of our fearful minds. Our souls make clear, in every moment, that we are okay, as we are, and still we convince ourselves we are unworthy and unlovable. Nature, in its easy alignment, invites us to recognize our own oneness with Source, and yet we have conditioned ourselves into this false belief of separation. Again and again we resist the knowing of our being, the truth of our intuition, the magic of our love. Why not see what happens when we stop resisting who we really are and what we are capable of when we let ourselves be?

We can't act cruelly toward others without being harmed by our own cruelty. When we pay attention to how we feel emotionally and physically when we succumb to meanness and hate, we realize how deeply connected we all truly are. If we refuse to be kinder and more compassionate toward each other even though it's the loving way to be, then let's remember that when we hurt others, we hurt ourselves too. Every single time. That's just one more reason to treat each other well.

Let's stop pretending we know things we can't possibly know for sure. Maybe just be quiet sometimes? Shutting up can often be the wisest choice, certainly better than spilling our ignorance all over each other.

But we've
been friends
for twenty years
is not a good
reason to stay
in an unhealthy
friendship.
Just because
we've shared
a past with
someone doesn't
mean we need to
share the present
with them too.

Healing isn't possible within denial and fear. It's only possible within openness and honesty, within our willingness to look at the truth of our reality, past and present, and to accept it for what it is without letting it define who we are right now. We are not our struggles or our heartbreak. We are not the actions we've taken or the assaults we've endured. Yes, our experiences influence how we grow and who we grow into. But ultimately, who we are is who we decide to be, because of and despite everything we've been through. Our power lives in choice. We can choose to face our pain without judgment, without letting it shut us down to our growth. If we decide to. And we can commit to loving ourselves through it all. As much as possible, no matter what. Love — self-love — transforms. This is how we create a safe place inside ourselves to heal.

We **live in a beautiful** and insane world. The media focuses almost exclusively on the insane aspects, and we in turn come to view our reality as only cruel, violent, and hopeless. We are not doing a disservice to others by turning off our TVs or shutting down our devices and choosing to meditate, write, go on a walk, connect with friends, or do anything we want that creates a bit more peace within the chaos. When it feels like the reality of our world is just too much, we can still remind ourselves to control what we can control, to return to our breath and this present moment, and no matter what, to keep seeking the beauty here too.

Sometimes
the very best
thing about a day
is that it's over,
and that tomorrow
brings with it
a brand-new start
with new possibilities.

Shame snakes its way into all areas of our lives, telling us that how we look or what we've done or what's been done to us needs to stay a secret. Yet the real secret about shame is that it can't survive being revealed. The moment we speak of the things we're ashamed of, shame's reins loosen, and its power dissipates within an air of honesty, ownership, and acceptance.

We think so much about what might go wrong if we take a chance on ourselves that we often forget to focus on what might go right. Our fear will never be the thing that walks us into the risk our heart is calling on us to take, which is why we have to give at least as much energy to our intention, to possibility, to the belief that we can create for ourselves whatever dream it is we're pursuing. While our fear leads us down its endless path of *no*, we've got to stay committed to our real, determined, more powerful *yes*.

We can hide ourselves because of our perceived flaws, or we can embrace the flaws. We can choose to see the ways in which our cracks add beauty to the world around us and the ways in which they enhance our own lives. We can choose to recognize that whatever makes us who we are is something to celebrate, not suppress. Without needing them to define us, we can begin to let our cracks give us a bit more definition.

We can't control whether or not we feel our fears, but we do have a say in how much power we give them. Let's carry our fears with us into the realization of our desires, rather than allow our fears to drag us away from the pursuit of them.

How can we truly love ourselves if we're not willing to be ourselves? Who is it we're trying to love then? Some version of who we think we need to be, a portrait painted by the expectations of others? No wonder we struggle with self-love; we don't have the *self* part down. Maybe we'll have an easier time loving ourselves when we find the freedom to be ourselves, when we encourage our soul to sing its own melody, when we let our body flower as it's meant to, when we dance away from the mandates of our minds. Sounds good, doesn't it? With intention and practice, it is possible. We can choose to un-become everything we've been told to be — or not to be — so that we can become everything we already are. We can choose freedom.

We have more control over our thoughts than we tend to believe. If a movie we don't like is on TV, we find a new one. If a song we can't stand is on the radio, we change the station. And yet, when we're thinking thoughts that make us feel like crap, we often keep thinking them. We lock ourselves into the misery. It's possible to change the channel on our thoughts too. Tune to a station that feels better, one rooted in love or creativity or beauty or anything that feels more uplifting. Why not practice this? Why not play with giving ourselves more good-feeling thoughts as often as possible? Not from a place of denial, either, but from understanding that there is so much more than darkness and pain here. Just as there is so much more than self-abuse and insecurity in our minds.

It's **easy to stick with teachers** or relationships or communities that no longer serve our well-being, that may even begin to cause more destruction than healing in our lives. We stay because we're afraid to leave the comfort of the known, even when the norm has become unbearable. We stay because we can't extract ourselves from the pressure to conform, even when our hearts cry out for freedom. We stay because we question our perceptions as false, even when our intuition won't stop declaring the truth. We stay because we believe we have nowhere else to go, even when endless possibilities live within the choice of moving on. We stay for so many fearful reasons; even so, it will always take just one courageous decision to leave.

It's vital to remember that no teacher or tribe provides the ticket to anything; you are the only necessary ingredient for your growth. I am the only necessary ingredient for mine. And, beautifully, we never stop growing, and our story never stops unfolding, no matter whom we invite to help us along the way. No matter whom we disinvite too.

Love has no agenda.

We are so afraid of hurting each other's feelings, we don't speak the truth to one another. We spend more time calibrating our words than being honest. And things stay the same. If we want to deepen our relationships, then we've got to stop tiptoeing on the surface. We have to find the courage to share the fullness of our truth, with kindness, empathy, and compassion, and to trust that by doing so we will invite a more meaningful connection with others and magnetize the people and relationships that will best support our peace and well-being.

It's important not to put off necessary conversations just because they're difficult to have (I'm constantly putting off necessary conversations just because they're difficult to have). And it's equally important to consider the timing of said conversations. It's best not to dissect your sex life during the Super Bowl or bring up your desire for couples therapy as you're heading out to a holiday party. It's hard enough for two human beings to work through their shit under the best of circumstances. And it's virtually impossible when we launch into a conversation at a bad time or with a bad attitude.

There's a huge difference between sympathy and empathy, between *I'm sorry* and *I've been there*. It's not that sympathy is bad. It's just that empathy invites a connection that sympathy simply can't. Sympathy says, *I feel sorry for you*, while empathy declares, *I am you*. Sympathy encourages us to find compassion, from a distance, for another's misfortune. Empathy demands we revisit our own pain in order to relate to someone else's. Sympathy requires our kindness. Empathy requires our vulnerability. How much more peaceful would our world be if we stopped to imagine what it's like to walk in each other's shoes? Or if we simply acknowledged it when we already have? Without judgment or having to agree with a person's choices, and without needing to have experienced whatever it is they're going through, we can always choose to empathize. We can declare, *I've been there*, or that we're doing our best to imagine what it's like to be there. Empathy is a conscious choice, and, like all conscious choices, it takes practice. The more we do it, the better we become at it — until empathy, rather than just sympathy, is our go-to response.

If we did no other thing
but align our choices with
self-love as often as possible,
we'd change our lives overnight.
We'd help change the world
overnight too, because love
of self always translates to
deeper love of others. Always.

Let's become
so devoted
to our truth
that to live it is
an act of freedom
and not rebellion.

We can't
stay committed
to our bullshit
and to our growth.
It's one or the other.

Our sadness
would not
feel so heavy
had we not
been trained
to believe
only happiness
was the answer.

Before we judge anyone for anything, let's consider how much of our judgment is rooted in our own fear, dissatisfaction, or insecurity in some part of ourselves or our lives. It's human to condemn others because of our own pain, but it's not wise or compassionate to do so. Let the impulse to judge be an invitation to go beyond our humanness, to that divine place within us that knows how to love and accept everyone, including ourselves, just as we are.

What does it look like not to take things so personally? It looks like being rejected by someone and understanding it's a reflection of their desires and not our flaws. It looks like reading an unkind comment on social media and reminding ourselves that what others think of us is not our business and that we will never be defined by their opinions. It looks like being grateful for solicited, constructive criticism instead of reacting with defensiveness. It looks like taking comments at face value instead of always believing there's an attack in there somewhere, and holding space for empathy and compassion when there is an attack in there. It looks like all those things and many more, and it feels a lot like freedom.

When we befriend
our own wounds,
we stop demonizing
the wounds of others.

The need to know why is another excuse we give ourselves to avoid moving forward, to avoid moving on. *Why did she make that choice? Why were they so cruel? Why did he lose interest? Why why why?* I can't answer some of the whys about my own choices, let alone someone else's. We can drive ourselves to misery trying to figure out why people do what they do (even when they actually tell us) or why life is the way it is. Or we can accept that we can't always know why, but we can move forward, and move on, anyway.

Let's encourage one another
and help each other out.
Give compliments and
recommend one another's work.
Let's not belittle or undermine
anyone else's achievements.
There's plenty of room for us
all to succeed, and a much
greater likelihood of us doing so
when we support each other.

When
our desire
for truth
outweighs
our fear
of change,
we make
choices
that serve
an open heart
rather than
a closed mind.

We long for love, all of us, to give and receive it. We long to be seen and appreciated and loved for who we are. We will never stop having this longing, so love will always have a hold on us, no matter how lost and unconscious we become, no matter how committed to hatred and war. Beneath our vast delusions, beyond the vile muck we deny or uncover, love waits, an always healer. Patient, willing, and ever ready.

One common barrier to loving ourselves is the idea that it's selfish to focus on self-love. But self-love is selfish. It is the most beautiful selfishness that exists. When we are steeped in love of self, we have big love to offer others in return. It's the only possibility. Love begets love. When we give ourselves over to self-love, we give ourselves over to love of others, to love of humanity, to love of our planet. There is no greater choice for all of us than for each of us to choose self-love.

It's not that
we don't know;
it's that we don't
believe we know.
We don't listen to
and trust our knowing.

How can we expect the world to change if we are unwilling to change ourselves? We hate the haters, judge the judgers, and refuse to forgive the supposedly unforgivable. We are hypocrites, most of us, comfortable condemning others for the same things we do. Like sheep, we follow; like wolves, we attack; like fools, we listen to the loudest voices, even when they scream nothing but ignorance and fear. We are lost in our desire to be like everyone else and paralyzed in our fear to be ourselves. We are desperate to feel safe amid our cries for retaliation and more wars. Where is the common sense? If you want to end war, be peaceful. If you want to know love, stop hating. If you want to find fulfillment, befriend gratitude. Real change isn't born from making the same choices, muddied with insecurity and fear, over and over again. We don't wrest ourselves from darkness by turning out our light. Everything just gets darker then. We can't single-handedly change the world, but we can change ourselves. Each one of us. With commitment and hard work, we will grow, and glow. And a single candle does wonders in even the darkest of nights.

When we commit to
our growth, we grow.
It's the only possibility.

Peace comes
in bits and pieces,
in intentional habits,
in the choices we make
that support the belief
that we are worthy.
And it comes
in the moments
we decide, no matter what,
to take care of ourselves,
and then do it.

I **escape plenty,** but less often than I used to, because I always return to the same place I left behind. Don't you? And it usually feels even worse than when I left it. Whatever it is we're running from doesn't go anywhere. It may not chase us every second, but it won't disappear, either. The truth remains. Which is why many of us don't like to be sober, consciously aware of ourselves and the planet. The whole truth lives in sobriety, and the whole truth is never pretty for any of us. It can, however, be tolerable. It can become something we're able to live with, even accept and honor, without always needing to numb ourselves to do so.

We have no idea what seeds we're planting as we create our lives, or if and when they'll be sown. All we can do is continue to create, despite the threat or reality of failure, and be aware and grateful when our courage has made way for a harvest.

Part of getting honest with ourselves is getting honest with how honest we want others to be with us. I have avoided so many difficult conversations because I didn't want to feel the discomfort of what I imagined the truth would bring. So I pretended everything was okay, and they pretended the same. And rather than facing the discomfort of a hard conversation, we sat in the discomfort of falseness for days or weeks or months or, yes, even years. It seems like it's easier to lie to ourselves about the difficult truths, but that's only the case if we don't consider the overall toll these lies, avoidances, half-truths take on us emotionally and physically. I bet, like me, you know how excruciating a hard but necessary conversation can be, and I bet, like me, you know the relief that comes with having it.

What we imagine to be someone else's reality is so often not. I'm no mind reader, and I've been wrong a thousand times about what I believed the other person was thinking, what they might say, how they might hurt me. We can't know what's true unless we're willing to face the truth in ourselves and make ourselves available to it in others. This is one path to freedom.

We have to take responsibility for how we choose to communicate. Are we showing up with love or with judgment? Are we open to seeing where the conversation goes, or are we rigid in our expectations? Are we committed to being kind or to being right? These choices count. They invite either connection or conflict.

We can live our lives determined to avoid failure, but in doing so we're certain to avoid taking chances that might transform our lives in myriad positive ways. We're also certain to prevent ourselves from learning how to handle failure when we inevitably encounter it. Sure, we fail less by not trying much, but we succeed less too.

By taking
ownership
of our
darkness
and pain,
we not
only serve
our own
healing
but also
grow our
compassion
for the
darkness
and pain
in others.
Our world
needs us
to love
ourselves
for real,
so we can
really love
one another too.

Rare and vital
are the ones
willing to face
and accept
the whole
truth about
themselves.

Sometimes
it's about making
different choices,
and sometimes
it's about accepting
the choices
we've been guided
to make.

It's an honor
to be invited
into someone's grief,
an honor
to be asked
to witness
the worst possible pain,
an honor
to be somebody
another somebody finds safe.

One beautiful thing about the heart is that its mandate is clear: *No matter what, just love.* It is within each of us to love all of who we are, without exception. Even the mind when it's anxious or cruel. Even the thoughts that are lies. Even the personality traits and bodily features we dislike the most. With willingness, and practice, we can love it all. We can love ourselves more completely than we ever dreamed possible.

There is an energetic shift happening on our planet right now. Do you feel it? A gravitation to simpler living, to the guidance of our elders and ancestors, to the wisdom of our indigenous cultures, to the power of food and breath and meditation, to the necessity of connection and vulnerability and time spent in nature, to the innate understanding of how powerful we are in our humanity and our divinity. The actions creating and being created by this energetic shift are tangible; we are seeing and feeling them in myriad ways. The energy itself, however, feels like a wild intangible, so huge and unpredictable I would never bet against it. Like an upwelling of support from God herself. Like a hurricane of hope, possibility, and transcendence. Like a monster wave meant to carry us from the abyss to shore. Yes, we are being held and guided. As long as we just keep on swimming.

When in doubt,
just Love.

About the Author

Scott Stabile is a passionate love advocate whose previous books include *Big Love: The Power of Living with a Wide-Open Heart*, *Just Love*, and *Iris*. He believes there is no force more powerful than love to create real connection and healing in our world.

Scott guides transformational breathwork journeys and leads personal empowerment workshops around the world. You can find his event listings at ScottStabile.com.

For new writings, check out his *Bigger Love* newsletter at ScottStabile.Substack.com.

A fairly consistent nomad, Scott lives somewhere in the United States.